☞ W9-DGF-443

Massachusetts
The Bay State

Tika Downey

PowerKiDS press™

New York

Published in 2010 by The Rosen Publishing Group, Inc.
29 East 21st Street, New York, NY 10010

First Edition

Editor: Joanne Randolph
Book Design: Greg Tucker
Photo Researcher: Jessica Gerweck

Photo Credits: Cover Bob Thomas/Getty Images; pp. 5, 19, 22 (bird) Shutterstock.com; pp. 7, 9 © Bettmann/Corbis; p. 11 © Amanda Hall/Robert Harding World Imagery/Corbis; p. 13 © Michael S. Nolan/age fotostock; p. 15 Robert Frerck/Getty Images; p. 17 © Robert Landau/Corbis; p. 22 (John F. Kennedy) Getty Images; p. 22 (tree) © www.istockphoto.com/Therese McKeon; p. 22 (flower) Courtesy of Wikimedia Commons; p. 22 (whale) © Paul Souders/Corbis; p. 22 (Dr. Seuss and Clara Barton) Time & Life Pictures/Getty Images.

Library of Congress Cataloging-in-Publication Data

Downey, Tika.
  Massachusetts : the Bay State / Tika Downey. — 1st ed.
      p. cm. — (Our amazing states)
  Includes bibliographical references and index.
  ISBN 978-1-4042-8111-0 (library binding) — ISBN 978-1-4358-3342-5 (pbk.) —
ISBN 978-1-4358-3343-2 (6-pack)
  1. Massachusetts—Juvenile literature. I. Title.
  F64.3.D69 2010
  974.4—dc22
                                        2009000541

Manufactured in the United States of America

Contents

The Bay State

Have you heard of Plymouth **Colony**, where the Pilgrims settled in 1620? It was one of the first lasting English settlements in the United States, and it is on **Cape** Cod Bay in Massachusetts. Massachusetts is in the northeastern United States, in an area called New England.

Before the Pilgrims came, Native Americans had lived in Massachusetts for thousands of years. The state's name comes from the Massachusett tribe.

In 1630, the Puritans founded the Massachusetts Bay Colony, on Massachusetts Bay. The fact that the Pilgrim and Puritan settlements were both on bays helped give Massachusetts its nickname, the Bay State.

These homes and this lighthouse sit on Cape Cod Bay, near Barnstable. Cape Cod is known for its seaside communities and coastal lifestyle.

Colonial Times in Massachusetts

The Pilgrims left England in 1620 to find a better life and **religious** freedom. Their ship, the *Mayflower*, landed near Plymouth Rock, on America's East Coast, and they built their colony nearby.

Life was very hard the first year, and many Pilgrims died. However, Native Americans helped the Pilgrims by showing them where to fish and hunt and how to grow corn and beans.

Over time, the Massachusetts colonies grew larger. They were still ruled by England, though. The colonists became unhappy with the laws England made for them. They wanted to make their own laws, but England said no.

Here Pilgrims are shown sharing a large meal with Native Americans in 1621. This meal became known as the first Thanksgiving.

Leading the Fight for Freedom

Have you heard of the Boston Tea Party? Colonists angry with English laws and taxes dumped English tea into Boston Harbor. It happened in 1773.

A few years later, English soldiers marched to Concord, Massachusetts. Paul Revere rode through the night to tell the colonists they were in danger. On April 19, 1775, the first battle of the **American Revolution** was fought at Lexington and Concord.

Many more battles were fought in Massachusetts. The colonies won the war in 1783 and became the United States. Massachusetts had already written a state **constitution** in 1780. It adopted the U.S. Constitution in 1788 and became the sixth state.

Paul Revere is shown on his well-known ride to Lexington and Concord here. Because of his ride, local men got to those towns in time to fight off the British.

Bays, Mountains, and More

Cape Cod is one of Massachusetts's most famous features. This narrow piece of land sticks out into the Atlantic Ocean then curves up at the end like a claw. It curls around Cape Cod Bay, the largest of the many bays along the state's coast.

Boston is on Massachusetts Bay. The Charles River, the longest river completely inside Massachusetts, runs along Boston's northern edge.

Western Massachusetts has the Taconic Mountains. You will find Mount Greylock, the highest point in the state, there. It is 3,491 feet (1,064 m) tall. Western Massachusetts also has the Berkshire Hills. These hills and the Taconic Mountains are both part of the Appalachian Mountains.

Many people enjoy boating and sailing on the Charles River, as shown here. The Charles River flows through 22 cities and towns, from Hopkinton to Boston.

Wild!

Massachusetts has warm summers and cold, snowy winters. The western mountains may get 6 feet (2 m) of snow!

Forests cover more than half of Massachusetts. Violets, mayflowers, and other wildflowers grow there. Beavers, porcupines, woodchucks, turkeys, black-capped **chickadees**, and many other animals live in Massachusetts.

If you are lucky, you might see a right whale off the coast. The right whale is Massachusetts's state **marine mammal**. This giant animal's name comes from the fact that it was the "right" whale to hunt. So many were killed that only a few are left. Today there are laws in place to keep the right whale safe.

The right whale is longer than a school bus, at about 50 feet (15 m) long. These giant animals eat only tiny ocean animals called plankton.

Bay State Business

Since Massachusetts is on the Atlantic Ocean, it is not surprising that fishing is an important business. Lots of clams and lobsters come from the Bay State. You might have eaten tuna from Massachusetts, too.

Farming is important in Massachusetts, as well. About one-third of all the **cranberries** grown in the United States come from Massachusetts. The state's farmers also supply milk, eggs, and even flowers.

Massachusetts's factories make all sorts of goods, from computers to airplane parts to books. Have you eaten candy lately? It might have come from a Massachusetts factory!

The cranberry is the official state berry of Massachusetts. These workers are harvesting ripe cranberries.

Beantown

Boston, the capital of Massachusetts, is nicknamed Beantown. Do you know why? Puritan women used to prepare baked beans every Saturday.

Boston became the capital of Massachusetts Bay Colony in 1632. Today, you can still see buildings from the city's early days, including Old North Church and Paul Revere's house. You can also visit Boston Common, the nation's oldest public park.

What else can you do? You can visit art and science **museums**, see a play, hear music, or see one of Boston's sports teams play a game. You can skate on the Frog Pond in winter. In warmer weather, you can ride the swan boats in the Boston Public Garden. There is a lot to do in Boston!

Boston is home to the Massachusetts statehouse, which was built in 1798. Its dome is covered in copper, which was then covered with gold in 1874.

Scituate Lighthouse and the Army of Two

Like many towns along the coast, Scituate (SIH-chuh-wit), Massachusetts, has a lighthouse. What makes it special is something that happened there in 1814. This was during the War of 1812, a war between the United States and Britain, fought from 1812 to 1815.

Abigail and Rebecca Bates, daughters of the lighthouse keeper, were home alone. Suddenly they saw an English warship in the harbor. Fearing the English soldiers would attack, the girls quickly picked up their **fife** and drum and played loudly. The English soldiers could not see the girls and thought soldiers were approaching from Scituate. The English soldiers left, and the town was saved. Abigail and Rebecca became known as the Army of Two.

Scituate Lighthouse was used to guide ships for the first time in 1811. The tower sits on Cedar Point, in Scituate Harbor.

Taking a Trip to the Bay State

More than 25 million people visit Massachusetts yearly. Some go to the beach. Others walk in the hills and mountains. Some come to enjoy winter sports in the snow. Others come to visit museums or see sports teams play. However, most visitors come to see the state's historic places.

At Plymouth, you can visit Plimoth **Plantation** and see how Pilgrims and Native Americans lived in the 1630s. Old Sturbridge Village, in central Massachusetts, is another place where visitors see what life was like long ago. You can go to Boston and follow the Freedom Trail. It will lead you to famous places from the American Revolution and later times. What would you like to do in Massachusetts?

Glossary

American Revolution (uh-MER-uh-ken reh-vuh-LOO-shun) Battles that soldiers from the colonies fought against Britain for freedom, from 1775 to 1783.

cape (KAYP) A piece of land that sticks out into the water.

chickadees (CHIH-kuh-deez) Small, gray birds with black caps and light-colored stomachs.

colony (KAH-luh-nee) A new place where people move that is still ruled by the leaders of the country from which they came.

constitution (kon-stih-TOO-shun) The basic rules by which a country or a state is governed.

cranberries (KRAN-ber-eez) Hard, red, sour berries.

fife (FYF) A small, flutelike instrument.

marine mammal (muh-REEN MA-mul) A warm-blooded ocean animal that has a backbone and hair, breathes air, and feeds milk to its young.

museums (myoo-ZEE-umz) Places where art or historical or scientific pieces are safely kept for people to see and to study.

plantation (plan-TAY-shun) A settlement in a new country.

religious (rih-LIH-jus) Having to do with a system of beliefs.

Massachusetts State Symbols

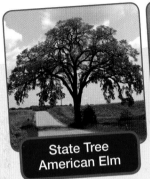

**State Tree
American Elm**

**State Marine
Mammal
Right Whale**

State Flag

**State Bird
Black-Capped
Chickadee**

**State Flower
Mayflower**

State Seal

Famous People from Massachusetts

Clara Barton
(1821–1912)
Born in Oxford, MA
Teacher/Nurse/Founder of
the American Red Cross

**Theodor Seuss Geisel
Dr. Seuss**
(1904–1991)
Born in Springfield, MA
Author/Illustrator

John F. Kennedy
(1917–1963)
Born in Brookline, MA
U.S. President

Legend

○ Major City

★ Capital

〜 River

Massachusetts State Map

Merrimack River

Gloucester

Lowell

Lexington

Concord

★ Boston

Charles River

Brockton

Taconic Mountains

Connecticut River

Quabbin Reservoir

Worcester

Plymouth

Hyannis

Cape Cod

Appalachian Mountains

Berkshire Hills

Springfield

New Bedford

Fall River

Martha's Vineyard

Nantucket

Massachusetts State Facts

Population: About 6,449,755

Area: About 8,262 square miles (21,398 sq km)

Motto: "Ense petit placidam sub libertate quietem"
   ("By the sword we seek peace, but peace only under liberty")

Song: "All Hail to Massachusetts," words and music by Arthur Marsh

Index

Web Sites

Due to the changing nature of Internet links, PowerKids Press has developed an online list of Web sites related to the subject of this book. This site is updated regularly. Please use this link to access the list:
www.powerkidslinks.com/amst/ma/